What's Wrong with the Microscope?

Fixing the Problem

Sheri Lang

I0807495

COMPUTER SCIENCE For the REAL World™

Rosen Classroom™

Published in 2018 by The Rosen Publishing Group, Inc.
29 East 21st Street, New York, NY 10010

Book Design: Jennifer Ryder-Talbot
Editor: Caitie McAneney

Photo Credits: Cover anyaivanova/Shutterstock.com; p. 4 hzdbzxy/Shutterstock.com; p. 7, 8-9, 16 espies/Shutterstock.com; p. 11 FeellFree/Shutterstock.com; p. 12 279photo Studio/Shutterstock.com; p. 15 freedarst/Shutterstock.com; p. 19 Triff/Shutterstock.com; p. 20 Videologia/Shutterstock.com.

Library of Congress Cataloging-in-Publication Data

Names: Lang, Sheri.
Title: What's wrong with the microscope?: fixing the problem / Sheri Lang.
Description: New York : Rosen Classroom, 2018. | Series: Computer Kids: Powered by Computational Thinking | Includes glossary and index.
Identifiers: LCCN ISBN 9781538353172 (pbk.) | ISBN 9781538324479 (library bound) | ISBN 9781538355251 (6pack) | ISBN 9781538352915 (ebook)
Subjects: LCSH: Microscopes--Juvenile literature.
Classification: LCC QH211.L36 2018 | DDC 502'.8'2--dc23

Manufactured in the United States of America

CPSIA Compliance Information: Batch #WS18RC: For Further Information contact Rosen Publishing, New York, New York at 1-800-237-9932

Table of Contents

In the Lab 5

What's a Microscope? 6

A Problem 9

Microscope Parts 10

How Do Microscopes Work? 13

Image Quality 14

Finding the Problem 17

Fixing the Problem 18

Testing It Out 21

A Great Tool! 22

Glossary 23

Index 24

School science labs have many tools for experiments.

In the Lab

In science class, we are learning about different kinds of science tools. We look at **containers**, such as beakers and cylinders. We look at safety tools such as goggles and gloves. We even get to test out magnets, which pull metal things to them, and thermometers, which measure temperature.

Today, my class is going to our school science lab. Science labs have many tools for doing experiments. We are going to look at one of the most important tools in science—the microscope.

What's a Microscope?

We learn that microscopes magnify an object. That means they make a small object appear larger than it is. The word microscope comes from "micro," meaning "small," and "scope," which means "view."

Compound microscopes are the most commonly used microscopes. They use lenses, or curved pieces of glass, to bend rays of light. This makes an image look bigger. Scientists use microscopes to look at things that are much too small to study with the human eye. Some microscopes can magnify objects to 2,000 times their size!

Microscopes are a common part of any science lab.

If you have a problem with a science tool, you should first **research** how to use it.

A Problem

We are each given a microscope to use. Then, the teacher gives us a **specimen** on a clear **slide**. We have to put the slide on a flat part of the microscope called a stage. Then, we have to turn on the light and look through the eyepiece.

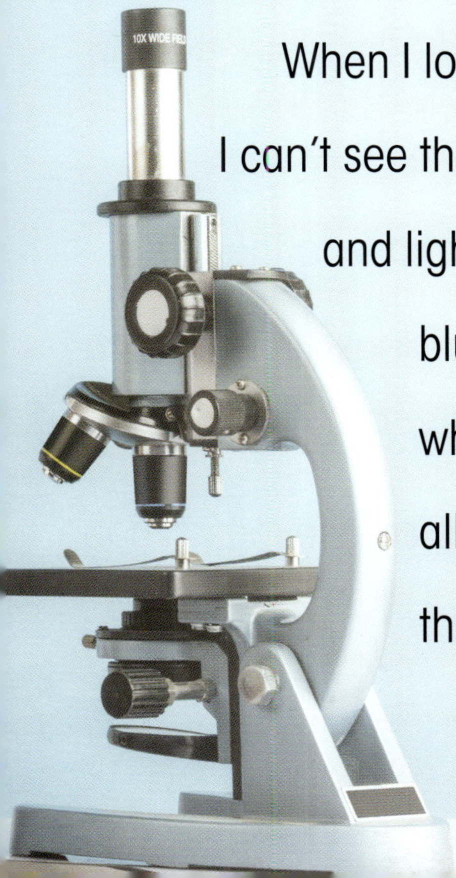

When I look through the eyepiece, I can't see the slide! I see the color and light, but the image is very blurry. I can't make out what the specimen is at all. What can I do to fix this problem?

Microscope Parts

I research the different parts of a microscope. I learn there are several basic parts to a microscope—the base, arm, and head. The base of the microscope, or the bottom part, has either a light that **reflects** off of a mirror to the stage, or an **illuminator**. The stage has an opening, called an aperture, where you put the specimen.

The arm connects the base to the head. The head has an objective lens, an **eyepiece** tube, and an eyepiece. There are two knobs on the microscope called the coarse focus knob and the fine focus knob.

Point to the part of the microscope where you would put a slide with a specimen.

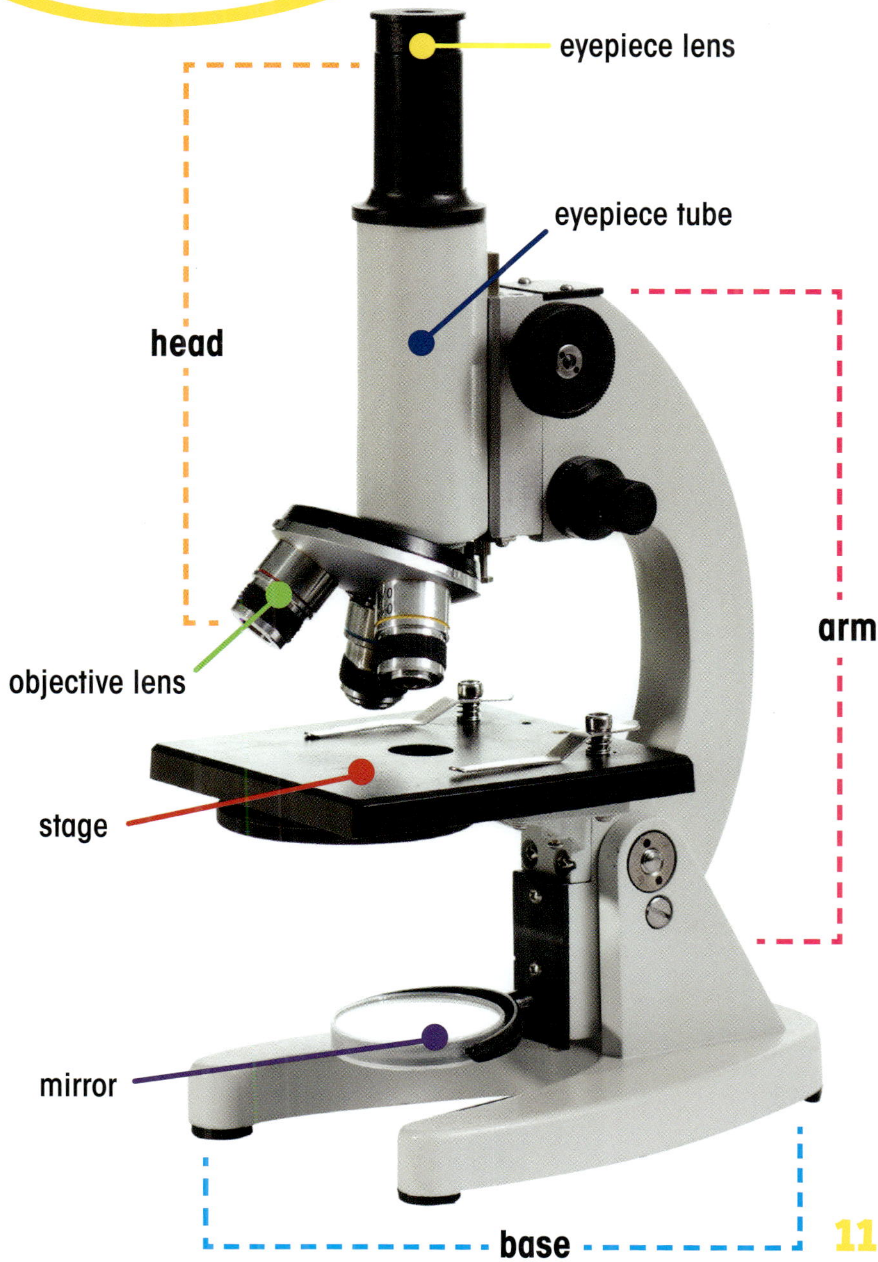

Learning how different parts of a device work together can help you figure out a problem with the device.

How Do Microscopes Work?

I need to learn how microscope parts work together. In some microscopes, the light reflects off of a mirror and onto the stage. In others, an illuminator lights up the stage from underneath. The stage holds the specimen. The light goes through the specimen.

Then, the objective lens, which is curved, receives the light and **refracts** it. This magnifies the image. The magnified image travels through the eyepiece tube to the eyepiece, another magnifying lens. I should be able to see a magnified image in the eyepiece.

Image Quality

Why is my image blurry? I know all the parts of a microscope and how they work together. Now, I need to figure out why the image **quality** is so low.

I use my school tablet to learn about what affects image quality on a microscope. I learn that brightness plays a big part. If you need the image brighter, you can change the light or illuminator. Another factor is focus. Focus is how clear an image is. The clearer the image, the more you can learn about the specimen.

Focus has to do with the distance of the microscope to the slide.

Finding and fixing a problem is called debugging in computer science. Debugging can be used anywhere—even in the science lab!

Finding the Problem

I look at my microscope again. I wonder if one of these two problems is the **culprit**. I look in the eyepiece again. The image is still too blurry to make out.

I think I have found the problem! A blurry image has to do with the focus. I need to find a way to make my image clearer. Then, I'll be able to study the specimen more clearly. Now that I know my problem, I can find a way to fix it!

Fixing the Problem

I think of a way to solve my problem. I learned a lot about microscope parts from my research. I remember learning about two parts that had the word "focus" in them. There's the coarse focus knob, which is bigger. Then, there's the fine focus knob, which is smaller.

I look in the eyepiece and turn the coarse focus knob. That helps bring the image into focus a little more. I use the fine focus knob to bring it even closer to a clear image.

The coarse focus knob is above the fine focus knob on this microscope.

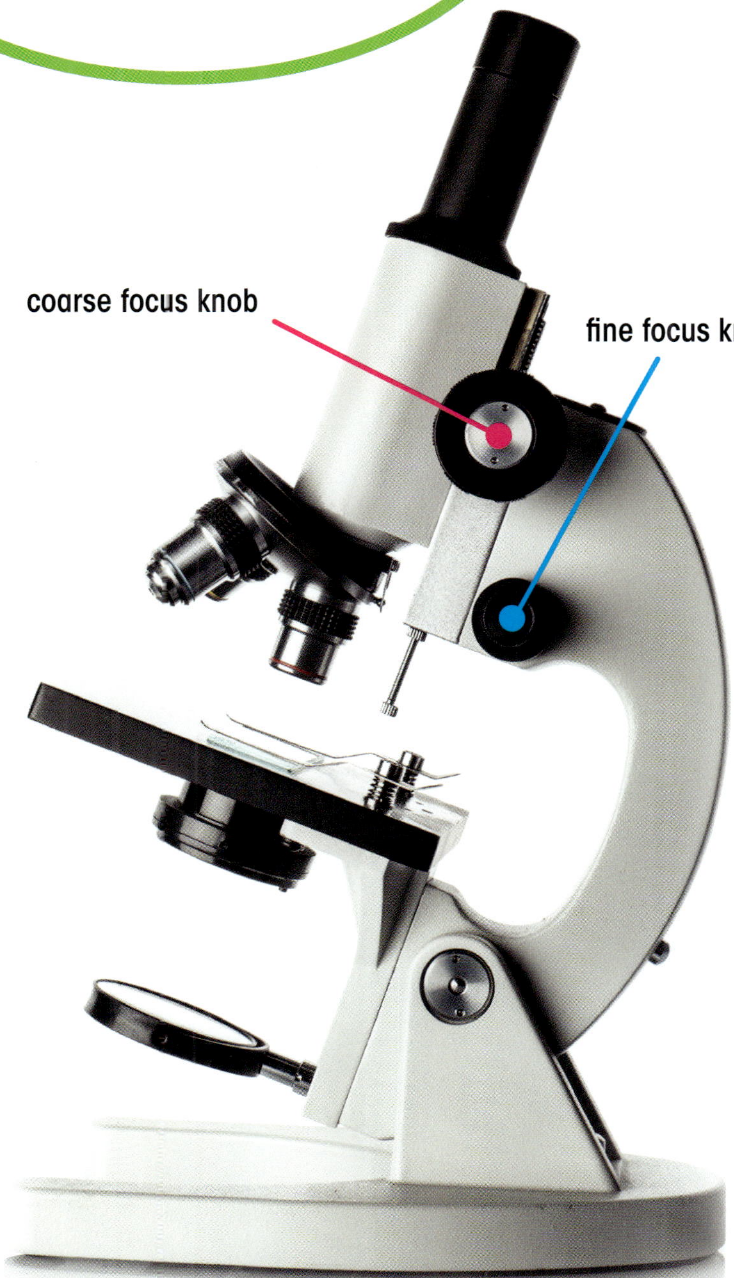

This is algae under a microscope. Algae are small, plant-like water dwellers that don't have roots, stems, or leaves.

Testing It Out

Now, it's time to test out my microscope. I take a good look at my specimen. My teacher wants the class to figure out what it could be. The specimen is light green. It seems to be very thin and stringy.

By looking at the slide, I guess that the specimen is a plant rather than an animal. I think it is a microorganism, or a very small creature, because of its size. I guess that it might be algae. My teacher says I am correct!

A Great Tool!

Microscopes opened up a whole new area of science when they were first invented. Suddenly, scientists could see organisms that were too small to study with the human eye. This deepened the study of **microbiology**.

Scientists use microscopes to study water and soil samples. Medical professionals use microscopes to study blood samples. They can look at **viruses**, germs, and cells up close. Microscopes are amazing tools used in many science fields. I feel like a real scientist when I use a microscope!